MW00413866

CLASSIC ROC
NUMBER 17

GOLDEN CLIFFS
COLORADO

by
Peter Hubbel

Introduction by Deaun Schovajsa

FALCON®

CHOCKSTONE®

A FALCON GUIDE ®

Falcon® Publishing is continually expanding its list of recreation guidebooks. All books include detailed descriptions, accurate maps, and all the information necessary for enjoyable trips. You can order extra copies of this book and get information and prices for other Falcon® books by writing Falcon, P.O. Box 1718, Helena, MT 59624 or calling toll free 1-800-582-2665. Also, please ask for a free copy of our current catalog. Visit our website at www.Falcon.com.

©1997 Peter Hubbel
Printed in the United States of America

1 2 3 4 5 6 7 8 9 10 VP 05 04 03 02 01 00

ISBN 1-57540-042-1 *Classic Rock Climbs* series
    1-57540-042-1 *Classic Rock Climbs 23: Lyons Area, Colorado*

Falcon, FalconGuide, and Chockstone are registered trademarks of Falcon® Publishing, Inc.

All uncredited photos bt Peter Donelan.
Cover photo of Ian Spencer-Green on Mr. Squirrel Places a Nut by Stuart Green.

Cataloging information on file with the Library of Congress.

CAUTION

Outdoor recreational activities are by their very nature potentially hazardous. All participants in such activities must assume the responsibility for their own actions and safety. The information contained in this guidebook cannot replace sound judgment and good decision-making skills, which help reduce risk exposure, nor does the scope of this book allow for disclosure of all the potential hazards and risks involved in such activities.

Learn as much as possible about the outdoor recreational activities in which you participate, prepare for the unexpected, and be cautious. The reward will be a safer and more enjoyable experience.

 Text pages printed on recycled paper

To Mayford Peery

TABLE OF CONTENTS

VOLUNTEER WORKERS BUILDING
THE ACCESS FUND'S TRAIL.

PHOTO BY: DEAUN SCHOVAJSA.

ACKNOWLEDGMENTS

This book would not have been possible without the help of many people. Some, however, went above and beyond the call of duty. Special thanks is due to:

Deaun Schovajsa for photos, footwork, proofing and doing the introduction.

Peter Donelan for photos, proofing, etc.

CT Traufield, my brother, for footwork, photos, proofreading and research.

Richard and Scott Berk for all their early North Table Mountain information.

Mayford Peery and the Access Fund for working together to provide us all with this climbing area.

and thanks to the whole crew at Chockstone Press, Thrillseekers Climbing Gym, and Mountain Miser.

Peter Hubbel
October, 1997

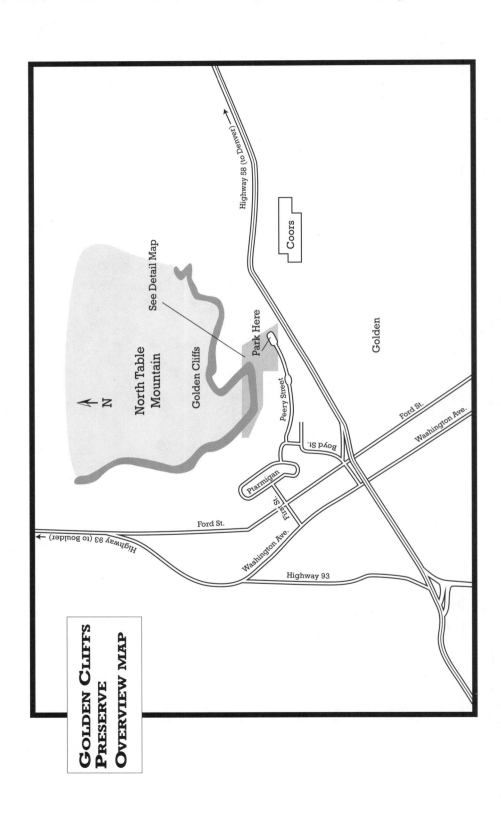

GOLDEN CLIFFS
PRESERVE
OVERVIEW MAP

N

North Table
Mountain

Golden Cliffs

See Detail Map

Park Here

Coors

Golden

Highway 58 (to Denver)

Peery Street

Boyd St.

Ford St.

Washington Ave.

Ptarmigan

First St.

Washington Ave.

Ford St.

Highway 93 (to Boulder)

Highway 93

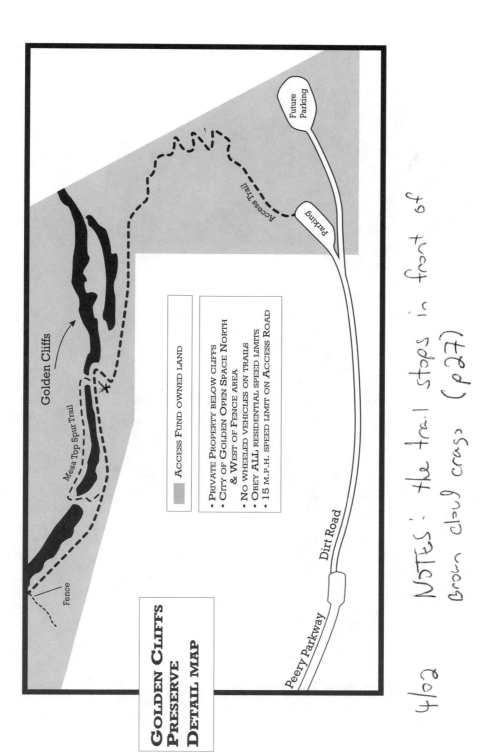

GOLDEN CLIFFS
PRESERVE
DETAIL MAP

ACCESS FUND OWNED LAND

- PRIVATE PROPERTY BELOW CLIFFS
- CITY OF GOLDEN OPEN SPACE NORTH & WEST OF FENCE AREA
- NO WHEELED VEHICLES ON TRAILS
- OBEY ALL RESIDENTIAL SPEED LIMITS
- 15 M.P.H. SPEED LIMIT ON ACCESS ROAD

Golden Cliffs

Mesa Top Spur Trail

Fence

Access Trail

Parking

Future Parking

Dirt Road

Peery Parkway

NOTES: the trail stops in front of
Brown cloud cross (p 27)

4/4

DEAUN SCHOVAJSA ON THE WINTERFEST WALL.
PHOTO BY: PETER DONELAN.

INTRODUCTION

GOLDEN CLIFFS

When Pete asked me to write an introduction to this guide, I was hesitant. Although I am very fond of Golden Cliffs and have spent dozens of afternoons climbing on the sun-soaked rocks or relaxing in their shade, I was aware that some climbers consider the area to be a small, unattractive chosspile, loaded with contrived, heavily bolted routes. While it's true that it doesn't compare to Eldorado Canyon or even Shelf Road, Golden Cliffs is undeniably one of the most popular climbing and hiking destinations along Colorado's Front Range. When combined with the fact that it's one of very few areas in the country actually owned and managed by climbers, Golden Cliffs becomes a significant locale—one that deserves an accurate and detailed tribute. The following is my perspective of the remarkable story of this highly popular crag and a chronicle of The Access Fund's dedication to preserving it, as they do all crags for the climbing community, as well as the public at large.

OVERVIEW   The Front Range is a treasure chest of climbing opportunities for the intrepid rock enthusiast. There are dozens of cragging destinations in close proximity to the Denver metro area. One of the closest, located within the city limits of Golden, is Golden Cliffs. The area, which has historically been known as North Table Mountain, is located on the rim of the mesa that bears the same name. Most of the climbing routes are on the escarpment along the south and west corner of the mesa. From this lofty vantage, one can view most of Golden below, including the huge Coors Brewing complex and the red-roofed buildings of the Colorado School of Mines.

Two significant attributes place Golden Cliffs apart from other nearby crags. One is its location. A prominent southern exposure ensures dry rock and comfortable temperatures when nearby canyons are shadowed and frigid. During a mid-winter cold snap or snowstorm, there are rarely more than three days in succession when the rock is not climbable. Busiest are the winter afternoons, when the mesa's balmy temperatures can lure even the professional couch potato out for a few hours of pulling and crimping. During the hot summer months, walls on the west face are shady and cool in the morning, but watch out because the heat can broil your brains by mid-afternoon. Spring and autumn days are usually superb.

The second—and perhaps more alluring attribute—is the sheer quantity of short, bolted routes below 5.11. No other Front Range area contains so many moderate routes in such concentration. There are numerous crack lines, some of good quality for the trad die-hard, but the main attraction is the many clip-ups.

For the most part, the routes here are well bolted. However, safety can vary from route to route. Some of the top anchors consist of unwelded cold-shuts, or cold-shuts dangerously worn from repeated toproping or lowering. Some replacement efforts (including the installment of questionable bolt hangers!) have been made by local volunteers but there is an ongoing need for maintenance. Climbers with experience replacing anchors should feel free to do so as the need arises—using, of course, only the highest quality equipment available.

HISTORY   Climbing began on the cliffs in the early 1950s. Many of the cracks were climbed in the last few decades before sport climbing came into vogue in the mid-1980s. Golden Cliffs saw a resurgence in popularity

MAYFORD PEERY (MIDDLE). THE MAN WHO GENEROUSLY DONATED THIS LAND TO THE ACCESS FUND.

at that time and by the beginning of this decade, routes were being established at a frenzied pace.

Much of the resurgent activity took place while the property was under the ownership of Mayford Peery. For nearly 30 years Peery allowed public access to the cliffs and approximately 85 acres of adjacent undeveloped land. However, in July 1994, he became concerned over liability issues and temporarily closed the area. The Access Fund contacted Mr. Peery and negotiations to re-open climbing and hiking access began. Almost immediately, Mr. Peery agreed to allow public access while a long-term plan for the area was being developed.

After several months of negotiation with Mr. Peery, the Access Fund accepted his donation of 28 acres of property that included the Golden Cliffs, a portion of the mesa above and below the cliffs, and an area at the bottom of the hill slated for parking. In addition, Mr. Peery provided an easement across a portion of his remaining property for construction of a road to the future parking lot. Pursuant to the wishes of Mr. Peery, this area has been named the Golden Cliffs Open Space. Rick Thompson, National Access & Acquisitions Director for the Access Fund, writes, "Thanks to Mr. Peery's philanthropic interest, he decided to donate the property to a private land foundation that could provide long-term stewardship to preserve the area in its undeveloped state, while facilitating continued recreational use for hikers and climbers."

In order to minimize impacts on the mesa, the Access Fund embarked on a two-phase plan that would 1) preserve the property as a permanent open space and 2) build a permanent parking area and approach trail that would sustain increased use. An application was submitted to the City of Golden that would rezone the property from its R1 or residential development designation, to C0, which is a conservation designation and prevents future development on the site. In addition, the application sought formal approval to construct a permanent access road and parking area. This application was approved by the Golden City Council in July 1997. Plans have been finalized to build two permanent toilet facilities, one at the new parking area and a second near the cliffs.

For construction of the new trail, which was a part of these plans, the Access Fund turned to local climbers for help. During a nine-day effort in the sweltering heat of August 1996, volunteers worked with a veteran trail building crew headed by famed trail designer Jim Angell, to construct a 3600-foot trail near the eastern edge of the property. From the parking area, the path winds its way up through boulders, shrubs and steep grassy slopes to the base of the cliffs. Future plans include the construction of a loop trail that will lead to the mesa top. Hikers and climbers alike seem to favor the pleasant passage and panoramic views of the new trail over the former one which was a grueling, steep hike along a prickly barbed-wire fence. The 170 volunteers assisting with the project did an outstanding job. On behalf of Golden Cliffs users: Thank you. An additional 800 feet of trail work remains; this work will likely be completed by the spring of 1998, at which time construction of the permanent road and parking is slated to begin.

The Access Fund's ultimate vision for the area entails the care and maintenance of this open space area by a group of local volunteers. As Thompson further writes, "A crucial aspect of this open space preservation effort remains unfulfilled: the formation of a community-based organization that will assume the day-to-day stewardship responsibilities of the property. This group, which will be known as Friends of the Golden Cliffs, will be composed of volunteer recreationalists and community members. By investing those who love this unique place most through the responsibility of caring for its future, the community and the land will best be served. With this long-term stewardship group in place, the success story behind the Golden Cliffs Open Space will truly be a classic example of grassroots preservation at its finest moment."

Sounds good. However, the transition from a neighborhood hiking hill to sport crag with 15,000 to 20,000 users annually is not without its problems. Tension among residents living along access streets, or with property just below the cliffs, has increased with the crag's popularity. Understandably, these folks resent the traffic. They've seen the carloads of earring-clad, tank-topped renegades, car stereos blazing, roaring by on their way to the rock. They worry about underage drinking in the parking area after dark, and some are angry about a perceived reduction in property values. Still others are troubled by the environmental impact of the steady stream of climbers and hikers on North Table Mountain's fragile mesa habitat. Whether or not these anxieties are valid or irrational, the Access Fund has systematically addressed each issue raised by local residents to the satisfaction of the city government.

Many residents, however, remain sensitive. Anyone visiting this crag to climb or hike should act accordingly. **Speed limits in the residential area are 20 mph.** The parking area opens at dawn each morning and closes at dusk each evening. At least for the time being, the Golden Police Department is managing the opening and closing of the parking lot and climbers should make sure that they are off the cliffs and out of the parking area before the evening patrol comes by. If you miss the curtain call, you may find yourself locked in for the evening. In general, the most beneficial thing that climbers can do for this valuable resource is to act responsibly, maintain a low profile and treat other users and residents with respect.

The funds required to maintain access to such crags as Golden Cliffs are considerable. In this regard, private and corporate donations as well as membership dues to the Access Fund, play an enormous role in the Access Fund's ability to provide funding for projects like the one at Golden Cliffs. These contributions, along with the efforts of Access Fund staff members and volunteers, are responsible for continued access to important climbing areas throughout the country. Please join today and do your part to preserve our climbing resources!

The Access Fund
PO Box 17010
Boulder, Colorado   80708
(303) 545-6772

It is equally important to recognize the man whose generosity and imagination ultimately allowed the creation of this very special place: Mr. Mayford Peery. Not only is Peery charitable, he has been an outspoken supporter of climbers in the face of many difficult meetings with the City Council and local residents over continued access.

On many weekends, Mr. Peery can be found working on the small pond near the parking area, or walking along the approach trail, picking up trash. He is a genuinely friendly man and for some reason he likes and respects climbers, perhaps more than some of us deserve. If you see Mr. Peery while visiting the crag, be sure to tell him how much you appreciate this unique area.

GEOLOGY, TOPOGRAPHY, ZOOLOGY AND OTHER STUFFOLOGY   The Table Mountains are two flat-topped mesas—North and South Table Mountain—located a mile east of the Front Range ramparts. The mesas were formed by an erosion-resistant, capping-layer of Tertiary basaltic lava, which served to protect softer layers of more erodable sediments. The lava was originally a continuous sheet that was later divided into the two separate mesas by Clear Creek.

The top of North Table Mountain is a gently rolling plateau covering about 1000 acres. The columnar lava composition forms prominent, vertical cliffs above the steep, 30° slopes surrounding the mesa. The cliffs where all the climbing is found are actually composed of two distinct lava bands. These bands are most noticeable on the southern face, just above the access trail. Only a few climbing routes exist on the lower of these two bands, which is of very similar mineral composition. Together, the bands have exposed vertical sections as high as 150 feet. On the west face, the upper band has sections up to 100 feet tall. The tops of these cliffs are perched almost 1000 vertical feet above the surrounding plains, creating a scenic landmark visible for great distances.

The lava flows are formally known as Table Mountain Shoshonite. It is a coarsely grained, crystalline rock in the lower to middle portions of the flows, while the upper portions are made up of finer-grained (and not as well consolidated) crystals. This results in a broken, crumbly upper edge to the stone cliffs. The lower to middle portions of the rock lend themselves well to climbing. Sharp, positive edges, shallow seams running vertically and horizontally, and a high friction coefficient on very compact rock create an endless variety of routes.

Many plants and animals make Golden Cliffs their home. Cactus, yucca, skunkweed and wild alyssum grass thrive in the semi-arid climate, as do the dominant shrubs of the mesa; wild snowberry, mountain mahogany, wild plum and skunkbush sumac. Currant and chokecherry are also well established on the flanks of the mountain. Scattered cottonwoods occur along intermittent streams in several places and occasionally in and alongside ravines.

Violet-green swallows are the most abundant bird using the vertical cliffs. The habitat is used heavily for breeding and the swallows do some serious damage to the population of flying insects. Several species of sparrows, towhees and warblers are common, as are turkey vultures, magpies, doves and nighthawks. More than 50 different species of birds have been observed on the mesa.

Mule deer, raccoons, coyotes, a variety of woodrats, mice and rabbits are the most common mammals sharing the mesa's diverse habitats. A few of the local residents claim to have seen mountain lions on the mesa as well! Lizards can be seen most of the year, sunning lazily or casually free soloing a 5.15 arête. The most dangerous inhabitant is the rattlesnake. Luckily, these timid creatures are more scared of us than we are of them. If you see a rattlesnake, please do not harm it, just walk away as if it were an enormous offwidth.

CAMPING AND AMENITIES Legal, inexpensive camping is a grim prospect along the Front Range.

Camping at the Golden Cliffs is not permitted. As mentioned above, the parking lot is patrolled at dusk each evening and the gated entryway is then locked. There is an RV campground in Golden, but the rates for a dry tent site are over $17.00 per night and the full-hookup RV sites are not usually available (some motels in town are about the same rate anyway). The nearest campgrounds are in the canyons west of Golden. Cold Springs campground on Colorado Highway 119 and Golden Gate Canyon State Park offer campsites and some backcountry sites as well.

The city of Golden and the surrounding municipalities offer a wide variety of hotels, motels, inns and bed and breakfast affairs.

For more information, contact:

Golden Gate Canyon State Park
Rural Route 6, Box 280
Golden, Colorado 80403
(303) 592-1502

U.S. Forest Service
P.O. Box 25127
Lakewood, Colorado 80225
(303) 275-5350

Golden Chamber of Commerce
1010 Washington Avenue
PO Box 1035
Golden, Colorado 80402
(303) 384-9145

The American Mountaineering Center
710 Tenth Street, Suite 110
Golden, Colorado 80401
(303) 279-3113

Just a five-minute drive from the parking area, Golden provides several drinking and dining establishments. The better restaurants include Mesa Bar and Grill, Old Capitol Grill, Tony Rigatoni's (in Morrison), The New Panda Restaurant, and Woody's Woodfired Pizza. The best of these, at least for the basic pizza and beer connoisseur like me, is Woody's. The standard fast-food fare is available in south Golden. Across the street from the American Mountaineering Center, Poor Boys Bagels serves up huge, delicious, fresh bagels and gourmet coffee. Safeway is the best bet for groceries. The extreme health nut may want to visit Golden Natural Foods. For anything else in the way of grub, drive east into Denver for a mind-boggling selection.

The Bent Gate is the local climbing shop, offering most items you may have left at home. Meyer Hardware will gladly take loads of cash for basic camping gear. For hard-to-find climbing items, or just for a good selection of technical gear, Denver and Boulder have some of the best shops anywhere.

SITES OF INTEREST AND OTHER ACTIVITIES   Of course, you'll spend an afternoon touring the Coors Brewery. The end of the tour teases your thirst with a sampling of frosty beverages. If you yearn for more, the Golden City Brewery is a few blocks away and you can purchase a twelve-pack of bombers to see you through the evening. While on the subject of alcohol, the Hakushika Sake brewery is an interesting tour. Artwork and photographs on display reflect three centuries of sake brewing tradition from Japan.

The American Alpine Club, Colorado Mountain Club and American Mountain Guides Association now reside in Golden and they share the American Mountaineering Center. The Center is undergoing extensive remodeling at the present time, but will be open to visitors in the near future.

Several museums and western historical sites are in or close to Golden. Movie theaters and shopping malls are best found in the Denver metro area. For extended bouts of bad weather, indoor climbing may be the ticket. Nearby outdoor climbing areas include Eldorado Canyon, Boulder Canyon, Clear Creek Canyon and Golden Gate Canyon State Park.

FINDING THE GOLDEN CLIFFS   From Denver and points east, drive west on Interstate 70 and continue west on Colorado Highway 58. After approximately 6 miles, enter the city of Golden and exit onto Washington Avenue. Turn right (north) on Washington and proceed about 4 blocks to 1st Street. Go right (east) to Ptarmigan. Turn right again and follow around to Peery Street. Turn left (east) and proceed to the end of the street, eventually passing through a gate. Here a sign is posted to explain access and regulations for the area. Follow the road to the parking area. The cliff access trail begins at the eastern edge of the parking area. From Boulder and the north, drive south on Colorado Highway 93 to Golden, turn left (east) onto Colorado Highway 58 then exit onto Washington Avenue after a half mile or so. Go right (south) to 1st Street, then turn left (east) and follow directions above. REMEMBER TO OBEY THE RESIDENTIAL SPEED LIMITS!

HOW TO USE THIS BOOK   The routes are described from right to left, east to west, beginning at Child Free Zone (p. 15). The trail from the parking area takes you directly to the Overhang Area (p. 29). Facing the cliff from the top of the trail, you'll look straight at *This Ain't Naturita, Pilgrim* (9) ✋.

GEAR   Quickdraws, quickdraws, quickdraws. Ten of them should suffice. Those routes which occasionally require pro in addition to fixed bolts are duly noted. Descriptions of trad routes include the size of pro likely to be encountered.

EMERGENCY
NUMBERS   Dial 911
or Jefferson County Sheriff's Department (303) 271-5304

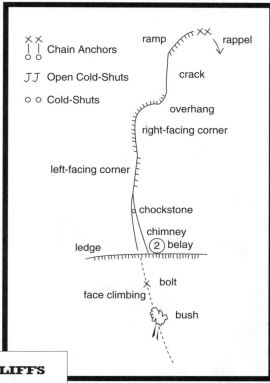

**GOLDEN CLIFFS
TOPO LEGEND**

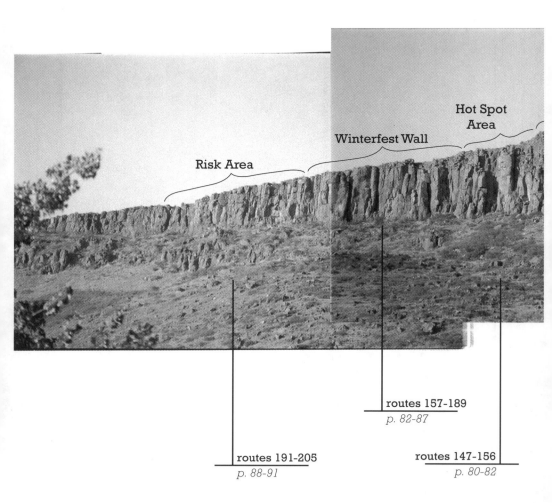

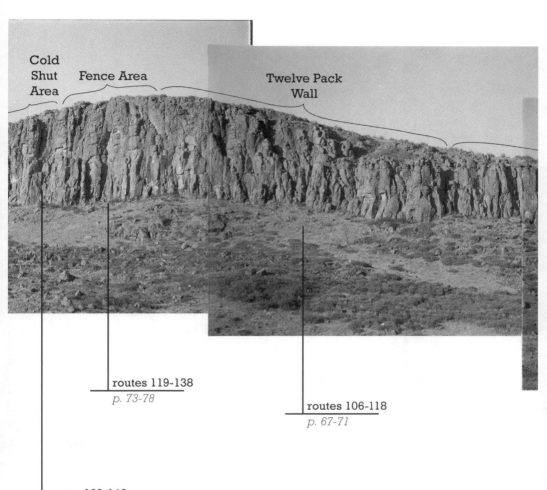

Cold Shut Area

Fence Area

Twelve Pack Wall

routes 119-138
p. 73-78

routes 106-118
p. 67-71

routes 139-146
p. 78-80

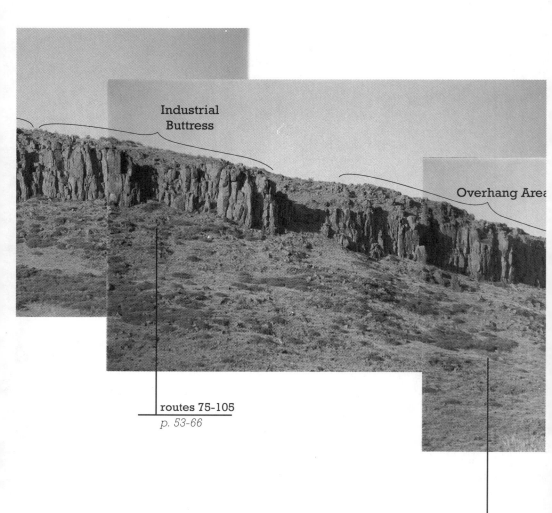

Industrial
Buttress

Overhang Area

routes 75-105
p. 53-66

routes 29-74
p. 29-50

a

Brown Cloud
Crags

Child Free
Zone

trailhead
access

routes 7-28
p. 15-25

routes 1-6
p. 15-20

SCENIC CLIMBING AT GOLDEN CLIFFS.

PHOTO BY: PETER DONELAN.

THE ROUTES

CHILD FREE ZONE (AKA PARKWAY CRAGS)

1   Carolina Direct

2   **Monkey Puzzle** (12b/c) 🖐

3   **Parental Abuse** (11c) 🖐   Steep, thin face on exposed column. Crux is halfway up.

4   **Unknown** (10a)

5   **Unknown** (10b)

6   **Big Loose Goose** (10a/b)

BROWN CLOUD CRAGS

7   **Louise** (8) 🖐

8   **Louise Arête Variation** (10a)

9   **Thelma** (7) 🖐

10   **Kid's Climb** (9+) 🖐

11   **New River Gorge Homesick Blues** (9+ R) 🖐

12   **The Virus** (12a) 🖐

13   **Thick Crust** (7)   Pro: To 4 inches.

14   **Top Rope Face** (11c)

15   **Big Dihedral** (8)   Pro: To 4 inches.

16   **Lemons, Limes, and Tangerines** (8) 🖐   Pro: Miscellaneous to 2 inches. Intimidating roof with big holds. One of the original bolted lines at the Golden Cliffs. Lots of fun.

17   **Protection from the Virus** (10c) 🖐

18   **Interface** (8) 🖐   Pro: #1 or #1.5 Camalot.

19   **Tenacious** (9+/10a) 🖐

20   **Volobee** (11b/c) 🖐

21   **Bullet the Brown Cloud (11a)** 👌

22   **John Adams' Adams Apple (8)**   Pro: To 3 inches.

23   **Killian's Dead (6)** 👌   Pro: To 3 inches.

24   **Deck Chairs on the Titanic (9+)** 👌   Classic. Popular route on a
       steep fin. Difficult right off the deck with a second crux up high.

25   **Variation (9–)**

26   **Windy Days (8)**

27   **Pee on D (8)** 👌

28   **Brown Cloud Arête (10b)** 👌

RENEE DOCKERY ON *HONEY I SHRUNK THE HEMORRHOIDS.*
PHOTO BY: DEAUN SCHOVAJSA.

CHILD FREE ZONE (AKA PARKWAY CRAGS)

1   Carolina Direct
2   Monkey Puzzle (12b/c) ✋

CHILD FREE ZONE (AKA PARKWAY CRAGS)

3   Parental Abuse (11c) ✋
4   Unknown (10a)

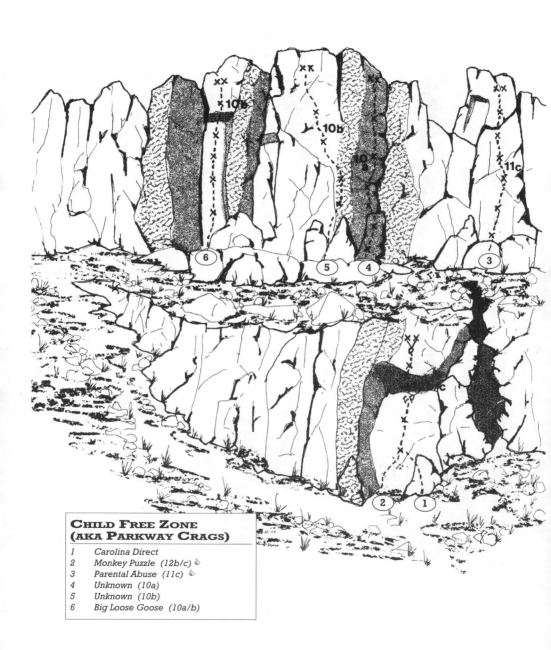

CHILD FREE ZONE
(AKA PARKWAY CRAGS)

1   Carolina Direct
2   Monkey Puzzle (12b/c) 🔥
3   Parental Abuse (11c) 🔥
4   Unknown (10a)
5   Unknown (10b)
6   Big Loose Goose (10a/b)

BROWN CLOUD CRAGS

7	Louise(8)
9	Thelma (7)
10	Kid's Climb (9+)
11	New River Gorge Home-sick Blues (9+ R)
12	The Virus (12a)
13	Thick Crust (7)
14	Top Rope Face (11c)
15	Big Dihedral (8)
16	Lemons, Limes, and Tangerines (8)
17	Protection from the Virus (10c)

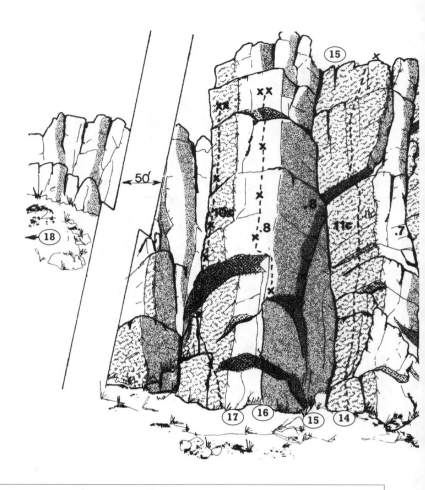

Routes 26, 27, 28 are in alcove. See page 24

BROWN CLOUD CRAGS

17	Protection from the Virus (10c)	
18	Interface (8)	
19	Tenacious (9+/10a)	
20	Volobee (11b/c)	
21	Bullet the Brown Cloud (11a)	
22	John Adams' Adams Apple (8)	
23	Killian's Dead (6)	
24	Deck Chairs on the Titanic (9+)	
25	Variation (9–)	
26	Windy Days (8)	
27	Pee on D (8)	
28	Brown Cloud Arête (10b)	

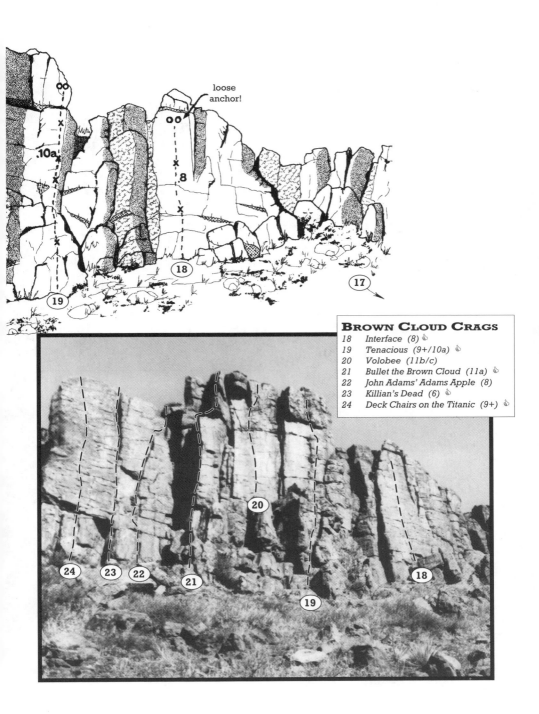

BROWN CLOUD CRAGS

18   *Interface (8)* 🔥
19   *Tenacious (9+/10a)* 🔥
20   *Volobee (11b/c)*
21   *Bullet the Brown Cloud (11a)* 🔥
22   *John Adams' Adams Apple (8)*
23   *Killian's Dead (6)* 🔥
24   *Deck Chairs on the Titanic (9+)* 🔥

BROWN CLOUD CRAGS

20   *Volobee (11b/c)*
21   *Bullet the Brown Cloud (11a)* 🔥
22   *John Adams' Adams Apple (8)*
23   *Killian's Dead (6)* 🔥
24   *Deck Chairs on the Titanic (9+)* 🔥
25   *Variation (9–)*
26   *Windy Days (8)*
27   *Pee on D (8)* 🔥
28   *Brown Cloud Arête (10b)* 🔥

4/22 trail stops
in front of 22, 23, 24

CLIMBER ON *BULLET THE BROWN CLOUD.*

PHOTO BY: DEAUN SCHOVAJSA.

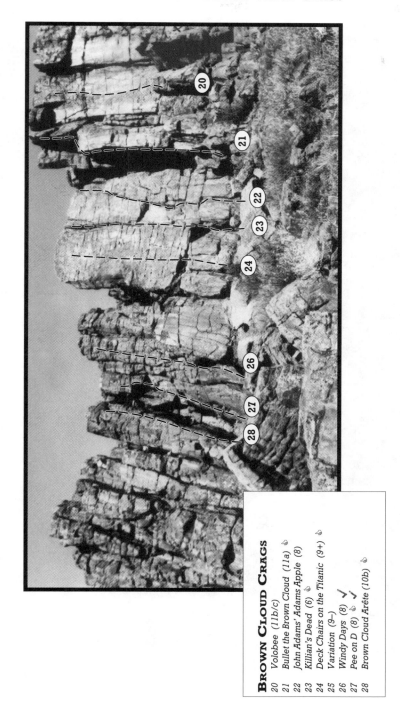

Brown Cloud Crags
20 Volobee (11b/c)
21 Bullet the Brown Cloud (11a) 🖐
22 John Adams' Adams Apple (8) 🖐
23 Killian's Dead (6) 🖐
24 Deck Chairs on the Titanic (9+) 🖐
25 Variation (9–)
26 Windy Days (8) 🖐 ↙
27 Pee on D (8) 🖐 ↙
28 Brown Cloud Arête (10b) 🖐

DEAUN SCHOVAJSA ON *MRS. HEN PLACES A PECK (5.12A)*.

PHOTO BY: PETER DONELAN.

OVERHANG AREA

29   **Pack o' Bobs** (7) ◊

30   **Another Unnamed Billy Bob Route** (7+) ◊

31   **The Fabulous Flying Carrs Route** (10d/11a) ◊

32   **Natural Fact** (7)   Pro: To 3 inches.

33   **This Ain't Naturita, Pilgrim** (9) ◊   Crux is thin moves on upper smooth face.

34   **Hellbound II** (9+/10a)   Pro: To 4 inches.

35   **Smear Me a Beer** (11b) ◊   This one is 11b if you climb the lower arête right on the edge. Most people stem into the left corner and make it a 5.9 chimney problem. Good route with some long reaches.

36   **Variation** (9+)

37   **Hellraiser** (9)   Pro: To 3.5 inches.

38   **Mrs. Hen Places a Peck** (12a) ◊   Great route! Overhanging face on thin holds and finger crack. Difficulties mount until jug edge below anchors. Open cold shuts at top, so don't climb above them.

39   **Here Today, Gone Tomorrow** (11d) ◊

40   **Variation** (9–)

41   **Mr. Coors Contributes to the Pink Stain** (9+) ◊   Pro: To 3.5 inches.

42   **Unknown**

43   **Handle this Hard On** (12a) ◊

44   **Tora, Tora, Tora** (11b/c) ◊   Pro: To 2 inches.

45   **Mr. Squirrel Places a Nut** (11c) ◊   Crux is lower face climbing. Very thin. Spectacular roof with positive holds.

46   **Off Line** (8)

47   **Corniche** (8)   Pro: To 4 inches.

48   **In Between the Lines** (9–) ◊

49   **Sidelines** (10a)

50   **Beer Drinkers and Hell Raisers** (8+)   Pro: To 4 inches.

51   **Beer Barrel Buttress** (10c/d R) ◊

52   **Top Rope Face**

53   **The Ground Doesn't Lie** (10c) ◊

54   **Unknown**

55   **Pigeon Pile Pinnacle** (10c) ◊

56   **Variation (11a)**   Original start.

57   **Project (13)**

58   **Don't Pout 'cause Yer Down 'n Out (8+)**   Pro: To 3 inches.

59   **Lying on the Ground (11d)** ♦

60   **D's Dry Dream (10a/b)** ♦   Inside corner with several lines of possible ascent. Much easier if you stay in the crack or stem off of back wall.

61   **Drinking Wine with the Chinese (9)**   Pro: To 3 inches.

62   **Umph (6)**   Pro: Miscellaneous to 3 inches.

63   **Hug the Butt (11b)**

64   **Henry Spies the Line (10a)** ♦   Pro: To 2 inches.

65   **Let's Wake Up Ronnie and Barb (9–)**   Pro: To 3.5 inches.

66   **Sleeper (8+)**   Pro: To 4 inches.

67   **Redrum (7+)**   Pro: To 5 inches.

68   **Kevin Spies the Line (6)**

69   **Table Top (10b)** ♦   Pro: To #1.5 Friend.

70   **Mind Mantle Arête (10b or 11b)** ♦

71   **Meat is Murder (8)**   Pro: To 3.5 inches.

72   **Unknown (8)**

73   **Unknown (8)**

74   **Unknown (8)**

BROWN CLOUD CRAGS

✓ 26   *Windy Days (8)*
✓ 27   *Pee on D (8)* 👐
   28   *Brown Cloud Arête (10b)* 👐

OVERHANG AREA

✓ 29   *Pack o' Bobs (7)* 👐
✓ 30   *Another Unnamed Billy Bob Route (7+)* 👐
   31   *The Fabulous Flying Carrs Route (10d/11a)* 👐
   32   *Natural Fact (7)*
   33   *This Ain't Naturita, Pilgrim (9)* 👐
   34   *Hellbound II (9+/10a)*

Brown Cloud Crags

28   Brown Cloud Arête (10b)

Overhang Area

29   Pack o' Bobs (7)
30   Another Unnamed Billy Bob Route (7+)
31   The Fabulous Flying Carrs Route (10d/11a)
32   Natural Fact (7)
33   This Ain't Naturita, Pilgrim (9)
34   Hellbound II (9+/10a)
35   Smear Me a Beer (11b)

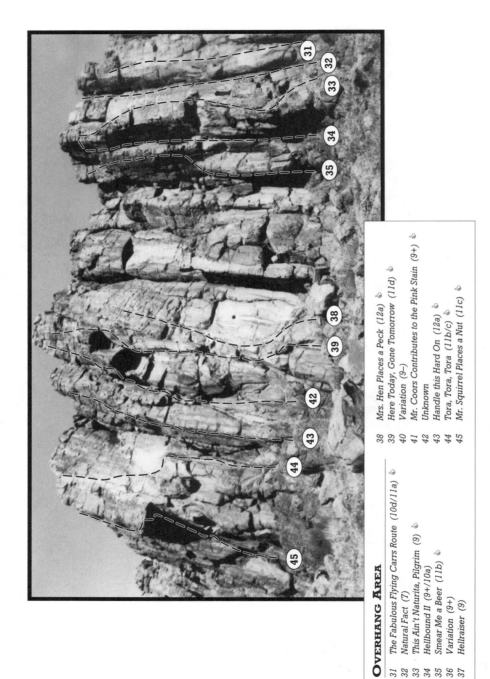

OVERHANG AREA

31 The Fabulous Flying Carrs Route (10d/11a)
32 Natural Fact (7)
33 This Ain't Naturita, Pilgrim (9)
34 Hellbound II (9+/10a)
35 Smear Me a Beer (11b)
36 Variation (9+)
37 Hellraiser (9)

38 Mrs. Hen Places a Peck (12a)
39 Here Today, Gone Tomorrow (11d)
40 Variation (9–)
41 Mr. Coors Contributes to the Pink Stain (9+)
42 Unknown
43 Handle this Hard On (12a)
44 Tora, Tora, Tora (11b/c)
45 Mr. Squirrel Places a Nut (11c)

OVERHANG AREA

33 This Ain't Naturita, Pilgrim (9) 🪝
34 Hellbound II (9+/10a)
35 Smear Me a Beer (11b) 🪝
36 Variation (9+)
37 Hellraiser (9)
38 Mrs. Hen Places a Peck (12a) 🪝
39 Here Today, Gone Tomorrow (11d) 🪝
40 Variation (9–)
41 Mr. Coors Contributes to the Pink Stain (9+) 🪝
42 Unknown
43 Handle this Hard On (12a) 🪝
44 Tora, Tora, Tora (11b/c) 🪝
45 Mr. Squirrel Places a Nut (11c) 🪝
46 Off Line (8)

OVERHANG AREA

34   Hellbound II (9+/10a)
35   Smear Me a Beer (11b) 🖐
36   Variation (9+)
37   Hellraiser (9)
38   Mrs. Hen Places a Peck (12a) 🖐
39   Here Today, Gone Tomorrow (11d) 🖐
40   Variation (9–)
41   Mr. Coors Contributes to the Pink Stain (9+) 🖐
42   Unknown
43   Handle this Hard On (12a) 🖐
44   Tora, Tora, Tora (11b/c) 🖐
45   Mr. Squirrel Places a Nut (11c) 🖐
46   Off Line (8)
47   Corniche (8)
48   In Between the Lines (9–) 🖐
49   Sidelines (10a)
50   Beer Drinkers and Hell Raisers (8+)

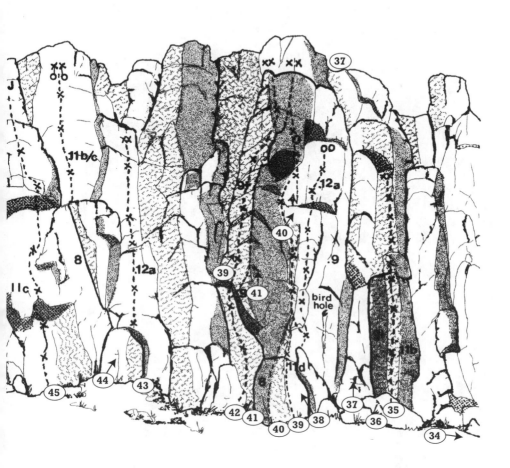

OVERHANG AREA

45　Mr. Squirrel Places a Nut (11c)
46　Off Line (8)
47　Corniche (8)
48　In Between the Lines (9−)

49　Sidelines (10a)
50　Beer Drinkers and Hell Raisers (8+)
51　Beer Barrel Buttress (10c/d R)
52　Top Rope Face
53　The Ground Doesn't Lie (10c)

ERIC BRAATON ON *IN BETWEEN THE LINES (5.9-)*.
PHOTO BY: DEAUN SCHOVAJSA.

OVERHANG AREA

50   *Beer Drinkers and Hell Raisers (8+)*
51   *Beer Barrel Buttress (10c/d R)* 💧
52   *Top Rope Face*
53   *The Ground Doesn't Lie (10c)* 💧
54   *Unknown*
55   *Pigeon Pile Pinnacle (10c)* 💧
56   *Variation (11a)*
57   *Project (13)*

58   *Don't Pout 'cause Yer Down 'n Out (8+)*
59   *Lying on the Ground (11d)* 💧
60   *D's Dry Dream (10a/b)* 💧
61   *Drinking Wine with the Chinese (9)*
62   *Umph (6)*
63   *Hug the Butt (11b)*
64   *Henry Spies the Line (10a)* 💧
65   *Let's Wake Up Ronnie and Barb (9–)*
66   *Sleeper (8+)*

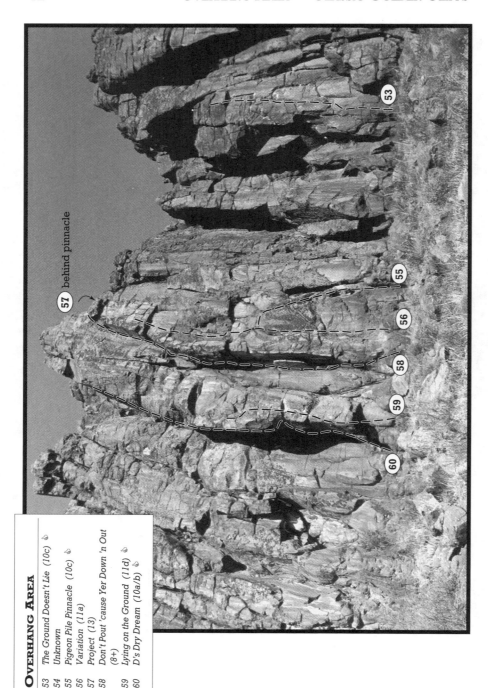

OVERHANG AREA

53 *The Ground Doesn't Lie (10c)* 🔩
54 *Unknown*
55 *Pigeon Pile Pinnacle (10c)* 🔩
56 *Variation (11a)*
57 *Project (13)*
58 *Don't Pout 'cause Yer Down 'n Out (8+)*
59 *Lying on the Ground (11d)* 🔩
60 *D's Dry Dream (10a/b)* 🔩

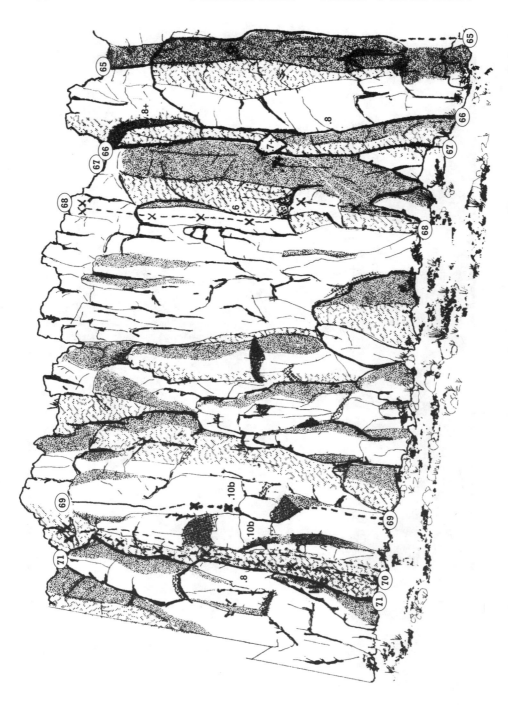

RENEE DOCKERY HALFWAY UP *HONEY I SHRUNK THE HEMORRHOIDS (5.7)*.

PHOTO BY: DEAN SCHOVAJSA.

OVERHANG AREA

66 Sleeper (8+)
67 Redrum (7+)
68 Kevin Spies the Line (6)
69 Table Top (10b)
70 Mind Mantle Arête (10b or 11b)
71 Meat is Murder (8)
72 Unknown (8)
73 Unknown (8)
74 Unknown (8)

OVERHANG AREA

68 Kevin Spies the Line (6)
69 Table Top (10b) ⬧
70 Mind Mantle Arête (10b or 11b) ⬧

OVERHANG AREA

70	*Mind Mantle Arête* (10b or 11b) 🖐
71	*Meat is Murder* (8)
72	*Unknown* (8)
73	*Unknown* (8)
74	*Unknown* (8)

INDUSTRIAL BUTTRESS

75	*Wazup?* (8+)
76	*Hodat?* (9–)

OVERHANG AREA

72 Unknown (8)
73 Unknown (8)
74 Unknown (8)

Peter Donelan on *Mind Mantle Arete (5.10b or 5.11b)*.

Photo by: Deaun Schovajsa.

DEAUN SCHOVAJSA ON *BRAIN CLOUD* (5.9).

PHOTO BY: DEAUN SCHOVAJSA.

INDUSTRIAL BUTTRESS

75   **Wazup? (8+)**   Pro: To 3 inches.

76   **Hodat? (9–)**   Pro: To 3 inches.

77   **Table Manners (11c)** 🔥   Pro: #1 TCU.

78   **Stoney Middleton (8)**   Pro: To 4 inches.

79   **Shadow of a Hangdog aka Fart Fingers (10a/b)** 🔥
Pro: To 2 inches.

80   **Brain Cloud (9)** 🔥   Beautiful straight-up arête. Tricky crux move midway up. This is the best 5.9 on the cliffs.

81   **Mandela aka Leaning Pillar (8+)**   Pro: To 4 inches.

82   **Major Bolt Achievement (11a/b)** 🔥   Pro: To 2 inches.
This one is sweet. Varied and sustained climbing with a nice roof to cap it off.

83   **Mournful Mullet (8+)**   Pro: To 5 inches.

84   **Shark Infested Waters aka Shark Attack (10d)** 🔥
Pro: To 2.5 inches.

85   **Feeding Frenzy (11d)** 🔥   Very thin, sustained climbing on a steep arête and inside corner.

86   **How Rebolting (7)**   Pro: To 5 inches.

87   **Sick Minds Think Alike (8+)** 🔥   Pro: To 4 inches.

88   **Top Rope Face (11c)**

89   **Darker is Better (7)**   Pro: To 3 inches.

90   **Thunderbird aka Light Beer (8)**   Pro: To 3 inches.

91   **Industrial Disease aka Dead Moonies Don't Sell Flowers (11c)**
🔥   Pro: Medium stopper. Awesome climbing. Dicey face moves down low lead to pumpy overhanging pulls up high.

92   **Flight 67 to Stockholm (11a R)** 🔥

93   **Blow Chow (7+)**   Pro: To 4 inches.

94   **Unknown (11d)**

95   **Polyvinyl Chloride (9+)**   Pro: To 3 inches.

96   **Left-Hand Monkey Wrench (7)**   Pro: To 4 inches.

97   **Nipple Phyle (6)**   Pro: To 4 inches.

98   **The John Roskelly Show (10a/b)** 🔥   Pro: To 3 inches.

99   **Noodle Factory (9)**   Pro: To 3 inches.

100   **Fast Boat to China (8)** 🔥   Pro: To 2 inches.

old Peery Street trailhead

OVERHANG AREA

74   *Unknown (10d)*

INDUSTRIAL BUTTRESS

75   *Wazup? (8+)*
76   *Hodat? (9–)*
77   *Table Manners (11c)* 🖐
78   *Stoney Middleton (8)*
79   *Shadow of a Hangdog aka Fart Fingers*
     (10a/b) 🖐
80   *Brain Cloud (9)* 🖐
81   *Mandela aka Leaning Pillar (8+)*
82   *Major Bolt Achievement (11a/b)* 🖐
83   *Mournful Mullet (8+)*

101 **Politicians, Priests, and Body Bags (10a)** 🔥 Pro: To 2 inches. Climb a short, narrow crack, then make an awkward move onto the crux face above. Need pro for the first 25 feet. Clip bolts after that.

102 **Heidi Hi (8)** Pro: To 3 inches.

103 **Toure Koundra (10a)** Pro: To 3 inches.

104 **Belly Up (8–)** Pro: To 4 inches.

105 **Scarlett's Pulse (8)** Pro: To 5 inches.

INDUSTRIAL BUTTRESS

75   Wazup? (8+)
76   Hodat? (9–)
77   Table Manners (11c) 🔖
78   Stoney Middleton (8)
79   Shadow of a Hangdog aka Fart Fingers (10a/b) 🔖

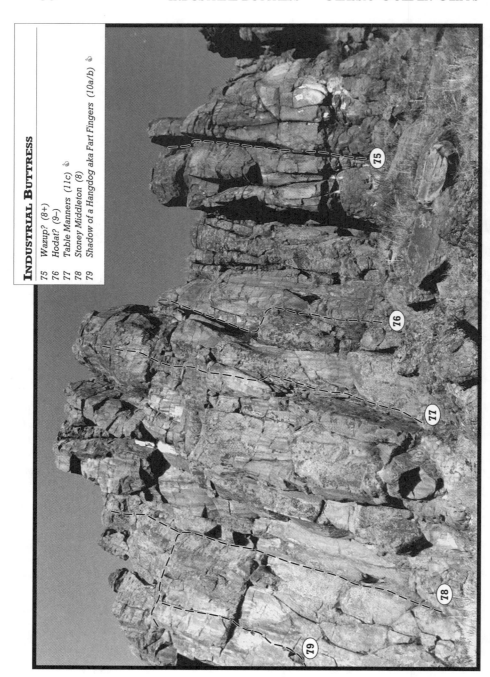

INDUSTRIAL BUTTRESS

82 Major Bolt Achievement (11a/b)
83 Mournful Mullet (8+)
84 Shark Infested Waters aka Shark Attack (10d)
85 Feeding Frenzy (11d)
86 How Rebolting (7)
87 Sick Minds Think Alike (8+)

old Peery Street trailhead (left)

INDUSTRIAL BUTTRESS

83   *Mournful Mullet (8+)*
84   *Shark Infested Waters aka Shark Attack (10d)* 🔥
85   *Feeding Frenzy (11d)* 🔥
86   *How Rebolting (7)*
87   *Sick Minds Think Alike (8+)* 🔥
88   *Top Rope Face (11c)*
89   *Darker is Better (7)*
90   *Thunderbird aka Light Beer (8)*
91   *Industrial Disease aka Dead Moonies Don't Sell Flowers (11c)* 🔥

INDUSTRIAL BUTTRESS

87   Sick Minds Think Alike (8+) 🖐
88   Top Rope Face (11c)
89   Darker is Better (7)
90   Thunderbird aka Light Beer (8)
91   Industrial Disease aka Dead Moonies Don't Sell Flowers (11c) 🖐

TOM JENSEN ON *FLIGHT 67 TO STOCKHOLM* (5.11B).

PHOTO BY: PETER DONELAN.

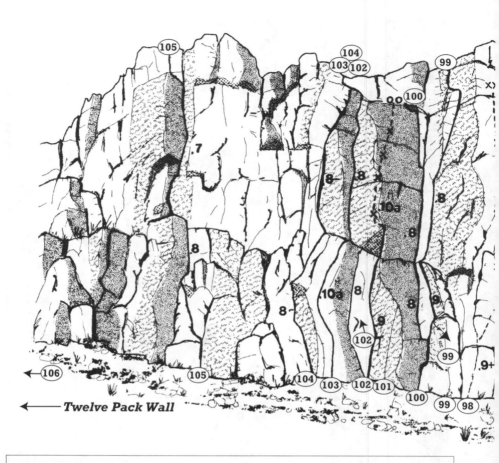

← Twelve Pack Wall

INDUSTRIAL BUTTRESS

89   Darker is Better (7)
90   Thunderbird aka Light Beer (8)
91   Industrial Disease aka Dead Moonies Don't
     Sell Flowers (11c) ♦
92   Flight 67 to Stockholm (11a R) ♦
93   Blow Chow (7+)
94   Unknown (11d)
95   Polyvinyl Chloride (9+)
96   Left-Hand Monkey Wrench (7)
97   Nipple Phyle (6)

98   The John Roskelly Show (10a/b) ♦
99   Noodle Factory (9)
100   Fast Boat to China (8) ♦
101   Politicians, Priests, and Body Bags (10a) ♦
102   Heidi Hi (8)
103   Toure Koundra (10a)
104   Belly Up (8–)
105   Scarlett's Pulse (8)

TWELVE PACK WALL

106   See You, See Me (8+)

INDUSTRIAL BUTTRESS

90   Thunderbird aka Light Beer (8)
91   Industrial Disease aka Dead Moonies Don't
     Sell Flowers (11c)
92   Flight 67 to Stockholm (11a R)
93   Blow Chow (7+)
94   Unknown (11d)
95   Polyvinyl Chloride (9+)

96   Left-Hand Monkey Wrench (7)
97   Nipple Phyle (6)
98   The John Roskelly Show (10a/b)
99   Noodle Factory (9)
100   Fast Boat to China (8)
101   Politicians, Priests, and Body Bags (10a)
102   Heidi Hi (8)
103   Toure Koundra (10a)
104   Belly Up (8–)

INDUSTRIAL BUTTRESS

101 *Politicians, Priests, and Body Bags (10a)* 🌣
102 *Heidi Hi (8)*
103 *Toure Koundra (10a)*
104 *Belly Up (8–)*
105 *Scarlett's Pulse (8)*

TWELVE PACK WALL

106 *See You, See Me (8+)*
107 *Unnamed (8)*
108 *Pump You Up (9–)*
109 *Spitfires and Funeral Parlors (9– R)*
110 *Chunky Monkey (10a/b)* 🌣

TWELVE PACK WALL

108 Pump You Up (9–)
109 Spitfires and Funeral Parlors (9– R)
110 Chunky Monkey (10a/b)
111 Love, Sex, and the IRS (8)
112 Honey, I Shrunk the Hemorrhoids (7)

113 Unknown (9)
114 Raw Fish and Rice (10b)
115 Unknown (10a)
116 Psycho Beta Buck Down (12a)
117 Briefcase Fulla Blues (9+)
118 C'est le Mort (9+)

TWELVE PACK WALL

106   **See You, See Me** (8+)   Pro: To 3 inches.

107   **Unnamed** (8)   Pro: To 3 inches.

108   **Pump You Up** (9–)   Pro: To 4 inches.

109   **Spitfires and Funeral Parlors** (9– R)

110   **Chunky Monkey** (10a/b) ☚

111   **Love, Sex, and the IRS** (8)   Pro: To 4 inches.

112   **Honey, I Shrunk the Hemorrhoids** (7) ☚   Pro: Miscellaneous to 1.5 inches. Classic. At one time, this was the most popular route at Golden Cliffs. Cool name, too.

113   **Unknown** (9) ☚

114   **Raw Fish and Rice** (10b) ☚

115   **Unknown** (10a) ☚

116   **Psycho Beta Buck Down** (12a) ☚

117   **Briefcase Fulla Blues** (9+)   Pro: To 2 inches.

118   **C'est le Morte** (9+)   Pro: To 3 inches.

INDUSTRIAL BUTTRESS

105 Scarlett's Pulse (8)

TWELVE PACK WALL

106 See You, See Me (8+)
107 Unnamed (8)
108 Pump You Up (9–)
109 Spitfires and Funeral Parlors (9– R)
110 Chunky Monkey (10a/b) 🔥
111 Love, Sex, and the IRS (8)
112 Honey, I Shrunk the Hemorrhoids (7) 🔥
113 Unknown (9) 🔥
114 Raw Fish and Rice (10b) 🔥
115 Unknown (10a) 🔥
116 Psycho Beta Buck Down (12a) 🔥
117 Briefcase Fulla Blues (9+)
118 C'est le Mort (9+)

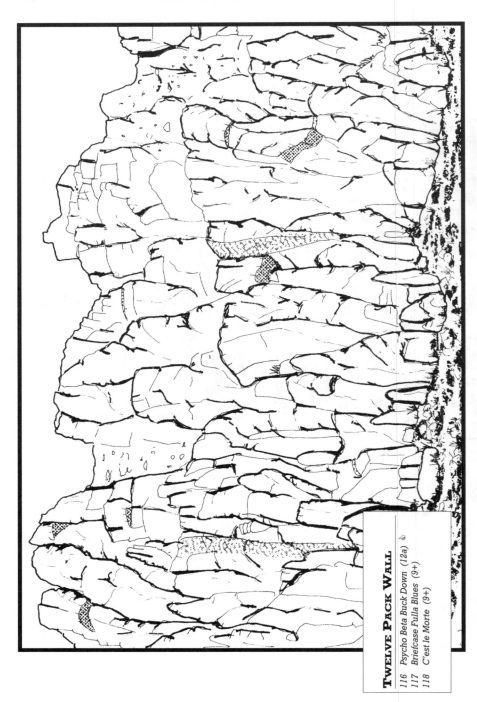

TWELVE PACK WALL

116 Psycho Beta Buck Down (12a)
117 Briefcase Fulla Blues (9+)
118 C'est le Morte (9+)

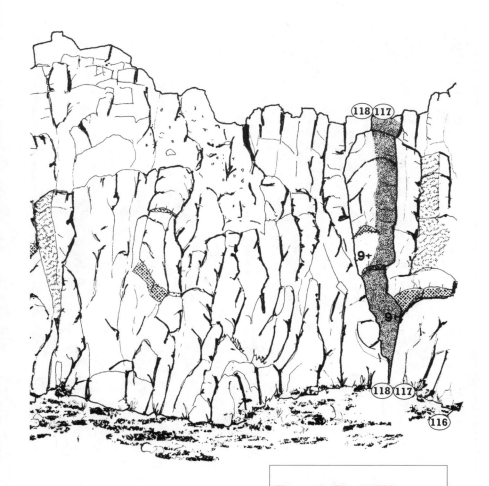

TWELVE PACK WALL

116 *Psycho Beta Buck Down (12a)* 🔥
117 *Briefcase Fulla Blues (9+)*
118 *C'est le Morte (9+)*

TOM JENSEN ON *WINTER WARMER (5.10C).*

Photo by: Peter Donelan

FENCE AREA

119 **Abortion Central (7+ R)**   Pro: To 4 inches.

120 **Power of Tower (11a)** ⚷   Pro: Wires to #4 Friend.

121 **G-Spot (8+)** ⚷   Pro: Wires to #4 Friend.

122 **Solar Panel (12d)** ⚷   With bolts in the center of the orange face, climb either side and stretch for the clips. Possibly the hardest climb on the crag.

123 **Unknown Corner (10b)**

124 **Foul Play (9)**   Pro: To 5 inches.

125 **Electrocuticles (12a)** ⚷   Sustained and difficult from the first move. Crux is low between the first two bolts. High quality!

126 **F.A.T.A.L. (Femurs and Tibias Alternating Laterally) (10a or 10c)** ⚷   Rated 5.10a for crack, 5.10c for stem. Thin crack moves with bolt protection. Nice line with consistently difficult moves.

127 **Klimbink is Verbolten (11d)** ⚷

128 **Unknown (10b/c)** ⚷

129 **Basalt and Battery (10c)** ⚷   Pro: To 2 inches.

130 **Insult and Flattery (12a)** ⚷

131 **Crash Test Blondes (9–)**   Pro: To 5 inches.

132 **No Gumbies (10d R)** ⚷

133 **Fenced In (9)**   Pro: To 3 inches.

134 **Winter Warmer Variation (10d)**   Straight up the right-hand line of bolts. Fun climbing, almost as good as *Winter Warmer* and just as long.

135 **Unknown (10b)**

136 **Winter Warmer (10c)** ⚷   Pro: Long slings. Tough moves right out of the gate with a crux on small holds about one third of the way up. Save some forearm to clip the bolt above the roof! One of the longest climbs on the hill, you'll need a 165-foot rope to lower off of the anchors. Best route of its grade.

137 **Pass the Basalt, Please (10b)**   Pro: To 1.5 inches.

138 **Unknown (10c)**   Pro: To 2 inches.

FENCE AREA

119   *Abortion Central (7+ R)*
120   *Power of Tower (11a)*
121   *G-Spot (8+)*
122   *Solar Panel (12d)*
123   *Unknown Corner (10b)*
124   *Foul Play (9)*
125   *Electrocuticles (12a)*
126   *F.A.T.A.L. (Femurs and Tibias Alternating Laterally) (10a or 10c)*
127   *Klimbink is Verbolten (11d)*

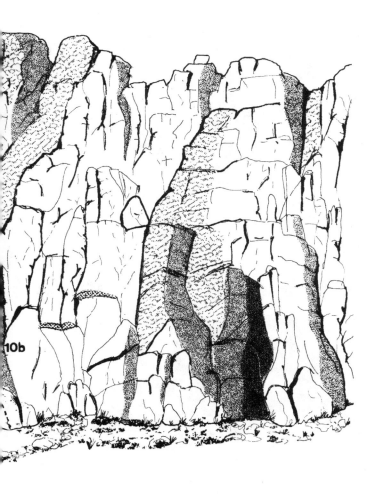

FENCE AREA

120 Power of Tower (11a)
121 G-Spot (8+)
122 Solar Panel (12d)
123 Unknown Corner (10b)
124 Foul Play (9)
125 Electrocuticles (12a)

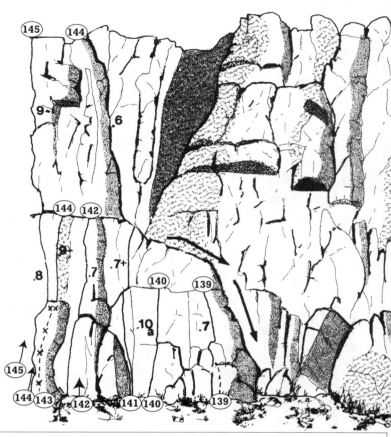

FENCE AREA

127 Klimbink is Verbolten (11d) ☙
128 Unknown (10b/c) ☙
129 Basalt and Battery (10c) ☙
130 Insult and Flattery (12a) ☙
131 Crash Test Blondes (9–)
132 No Gumbies (10d R) ☙
133 Fenced In (9)
134 Winter Warmer Variation (10d)
135 Unknown (10b)
136 Winter Warmer (10c) ☙

137 Pass the Basalt, Please (10b)
138 Unknown (10c)

COLD SHUT AREA

139 For Love of Mother Not (7)
140 Mechanically Inept (10a)
141 The Conundrum (7)
142 Unnamed (7)
143 Unknown (10b or 11a)
144 Unknown (9–)
145 Shut Down, Plugged Up, and Cold to Boot (9–)

COLD SHUT AREA

139 **For Love of Mother Not (7)** Pro: To 3 inches.

140 **Mechanically Inept (10a)** Pro: To 2 inches.

141 **The Conundrum (7)** Pro: To 5 inches.

142 **Unnamed (7)** Pro: To 4 inches.

143 **Unknown (10b or 11a)**

144 **Unknown (9–)** Pro: To 3 inches.

145 **Shut Down, Plugged Up, and Cold to Boot (9–)**
Pro: To 3 inches.

146 **Unknown (11a)**

COLD SHUT AREA

141 The Conundrum (7)
142 Unnamed (7)
143 Unknown (10b or 11a)
144 Unknown (9−)
145 Shut Down, Plugged Up, and Cold to Boot (9−)
146 Unknown (11a)

HOT SPOT AREA

147 Nine to Five (9+)
148 Disappearing Man (10d)
149 Honed to the Bone (Not!) (9)
150 The World thru a Bottle (10a)
151 Widespread Selfishness (12b)
152 The Crack and Face Route (10d)
153 A Quark for Quayle (9+)
154 Crowbar Cowboy (10a or 11a)
155 Dumb Politicians (10a)

HOT SPOT AREA

149 Honed to the Bone (Not!) (9)
150 The World thru a Bottle (10a)
151 Widespread Selfishness (12b) ✎
152 The Crack and Face Route (10d) ✎
153 A Quark for Quayle (9+)
154 Crowbar Cowboy (10a or 11a)
155 Dumb Politicians (10a)
156 Quayle Eats Bush (8+)

WINTERFEST WALL

157 Unnamed (9 or 11a) ✎
158 Whole Lotta Drunk (10d) ✎

HOT SPOT AREA

147 Nine to Five (9+) ♦ Actually the first pitch of a two-pitch line. Lots of varied moves with two distinct 5.9 cruxes.

148 Disappearing Man (10d) ♦

149 Honed to the Bone (Not!) (9) Pro: To 3 inches.

150 The World thru a Bottle (10a) Pro: To 2.5 inches.

151 Widespread Selfishness (12b) ♦ Pro: #2 Friend. Thin balancey moves on a smooth, slightly overhanging face. Crux is low, but climbing above is sustained.

152 The Crack and Face Route (10d) ♦ Pro: Stoppers to #3 Friend. Excellent quality. Difficult low, but the crux is climbing up the face in the mid-section of the route on sharp, positive edges.

153 A Quark for Quayle (9+) Pro: To 3.5 inches.

154 Crowbar Cowboy (10a or 11a)

155 Dumb Politicians (10a) Pro: To 3 inches.

156 Quayle Eats Bush (8+) Pro: To 3 inches.

WINTERFEST WALL

157 Unnamed (9 or 11a) ♦

158 Whole Lotta Drunk (10d) ♦ Short route with a single crux move. Enjoyable climbing and probably easier than its grade.

159 Jell-O Brand Napalm (9+ R) Pro: To 4 inches.

160 The Resolution (11c) ♦ Wriggle up and clip the first bolt. Make a hard move and hang on while you attempt the heinous second clip. The climbing eases above, but beware of the pump!

161 The Dissolution (11c) ♦

162 Thin Lizzie (9+/10a) Pro: To 3.5 inches.

163 Back to the Bayou aka Leaning Pillar (10c) ♦

164 Left Side of the Leaning Pillar (10d) ♦

165 Generica (10d)

166 Under the Wire (10a) ♦

167 The Consolation (10a) Pro: To 3 inches.

168 Unknown (10a)

169 An Artichoke (10d) ♦

170 Silver Bullet (10b/c) ♦ This popular route thwarts many first-time ascentionists with a devious crux in the steep corner, halfway up.

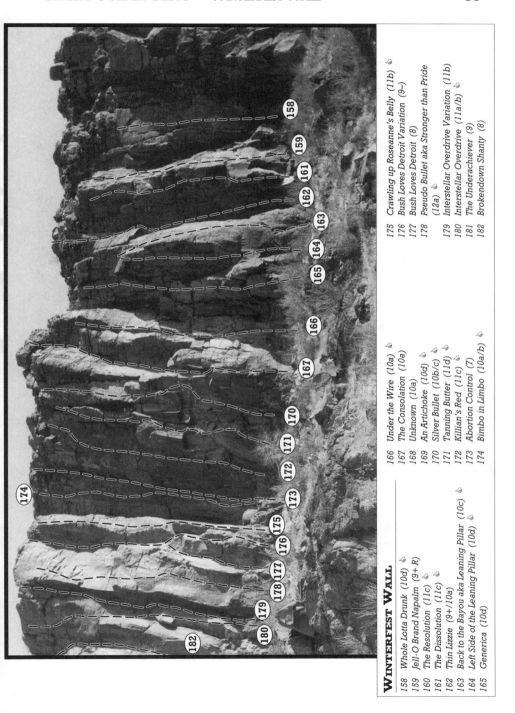

WINTERFEST WALL

158 Whole Lotta Drunk (10d)
159 Jell-O Brand Napalm (9+ R)
160 The Resolution (11c)
161 The Dissolution (11c)
162 Thin Lizzie (9+/10a)
163 Back to the Bayou aka Leaning Pillar (10c)
164 Left Side of the Leaning Pillar (10d)
165 Generica (10d)

166 Under the Wire (10a)
167 The Consolation (10a)
168 Unknown (10a)
169 An Artichoke (10d)
170 Silver Bullet (10b/c)
171 Tanning Butter (11d)
172 Killian's Red (11c)
173 Abortion Control (7)
174 Bimbo in Limbo (10a/b)

175 Crawling up Roseanne's Belly (11b)
176 Bush Loves Detroit Variation (9−)
177 Bush Loves Detroit (8)
178 Pseudo Bullet aka Stronger than Pride (12a)
179 Interstellar Overdrive Variation (11b)
180 Interstellar Overdrive (11a/b)
181 The Underachiever (9)
182 Brokendown Shanty (8)

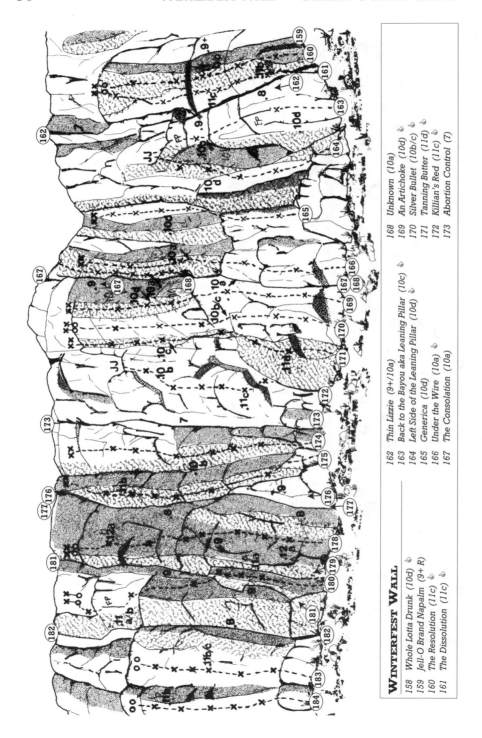

WINTERFEST WALL

158 *Whole Lotta Drunk (10d)* 🪝
159 *Jell-O Brand Napalm (9+ R)* 🪝
160 *The Resolution (11c)* 🪝
161 *The Dissolution (11c)* 🪝

162 *Thin Lizzie (9+/10a)*
163 *Back to the Bayou aka Leaning Pillar (10c)* 🪝
164 *Left Side of the Leaning Pillar (10d)* 🪝
165 *Generica (10d)*
166 *Under the Wire (10a)* 🪝
167 *The Consolation (10a)*

168 *Unknown (10a)*
169 *An Artichoke (10d)* 🪝
170 *Silver Bullet (10b/c)* 🪝
171 *Tanning Butter (11d)* 🪝
172 *Killian's Red (11c)* 🪝
173 *Abortion Control (7)*

WINTERFEST WALL

174 Bimbo in Limbo (10a/b) &
175 Crawling up Roseanne's Belly (11b) &
176 Bush Loves Detroit Variation (9—)
177 Bush Loves Detroit (8)
178 Pseudo Bullet aka Stronger than Pride (12a)

179 Interstellar Overdrive Variation (11b)
180 Interstellar Overdrive (11a/b) &
181 The Underachiever (9)
182 Brokendown Shanty (8)
182 Brokendown Shanty (8)
183 Driving over Stella (11b/c) &
184 Rebel Yell (11b) &
185 Too Dumb to Sleep In (8)

186 Unnamed (8+)
187 Sunset Aréte (11a) &
188 Photo Art (11a R)
189 Dweeb (9+)

RISK AREA

191 Sinister Minister of Evil (5.11d)
192 Baby Beeper (10b) &

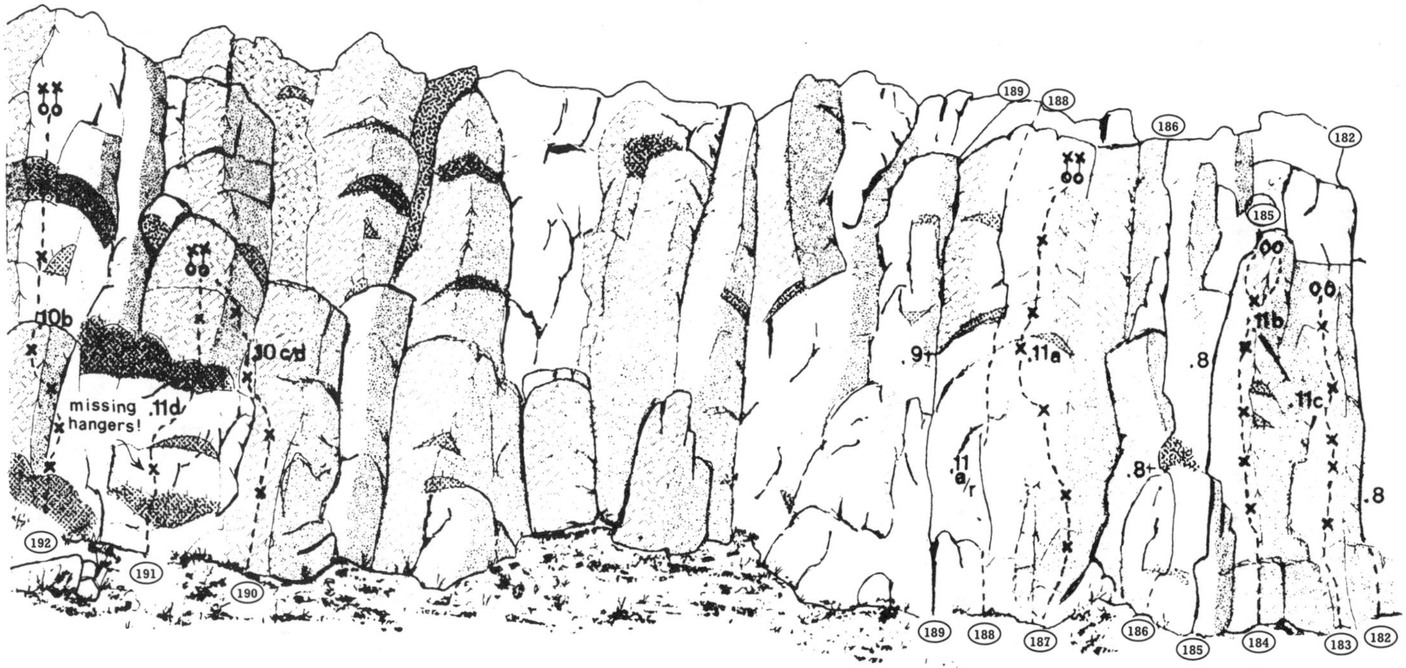

171   **Tanning Butter (11d)** ✍

172   **Killian's Red (11c)** ✍   Another inobvious sequence makes this one tough to send on a first attempt. Killer route though!

173   **Abortion Control (7)**   Pro: To 4 inches.

174   **Bimbo in Limbo (10a/b)** ✍

175   **Crawling up Roseanne's Belly (11b)** ✍   This one has some steep friction and a noticeable lack of finger friendly edges. Unusual for this area, but high quality just the same.

176   **Bush Loves Detroit Variation (9–)**   Pro: To 3 inches.

177   **Bush Loves Detroit (8)**   Pro: To 3 inches.

178   **Pseudo Bullet aka Stronger than Pride (12a)** ✍   Two 12a cruxes make this one interesting. The first one is low on the narrow fin. The second is high on the blank overhanging face. Good luck!

179   **Interstellar Overdrive Variation (11b)** ✍   Pro: To 2.5 inches.

180   **Interstellar Overdrive (11a/b)** ✍   Stretch your ankles well and slap on some sticky rubber for this stemming nightmare. Stays hard above corner. Fun?

181   **The Underachiever (9)**   Pro: To 2.5 inches.

182   **Brokendown Shanty (8)**   Pro: To 3 inches.

183   **Driving over Stella (11b/c)** ✍   This is a rad line on the low west-most column of the west face. Some slopey pulls make up the crux on this extraordinary line.

184   **Rebel Yell (11b)** ✍   Sweet! Start a steep face with some long reaches, gain the arête and soon the climbing relaxes a bit.

185   **Too Dumb to Sleep In (8)**   Pro: To 4 inches.

186   **Unnamed (8+)**   Pro: To 3 inches.

187   **Sunset Arête (11a)** ✍   Work back and forth between the face and the arête. One of the most aesthetic lines on the cliff. Holds about one-third of the way to the anchors. Best route of its grade ! Rated 11b if you climb the lower arête right on the edge. Most people stem into the left corner and make it a 5.9 chimney problem. Good route with some long reaches. Thin crack moves with bolt protection. Nice line with consistently difficult moves. Climbing above is sustained. Short route with a single crux move. Enjoyable climbing and probably easier than it's grade.

188   **Photo Art (11a R)**   Pro: RPs.

189   **Dweeb (9+)**   Pro: To 3 inches.

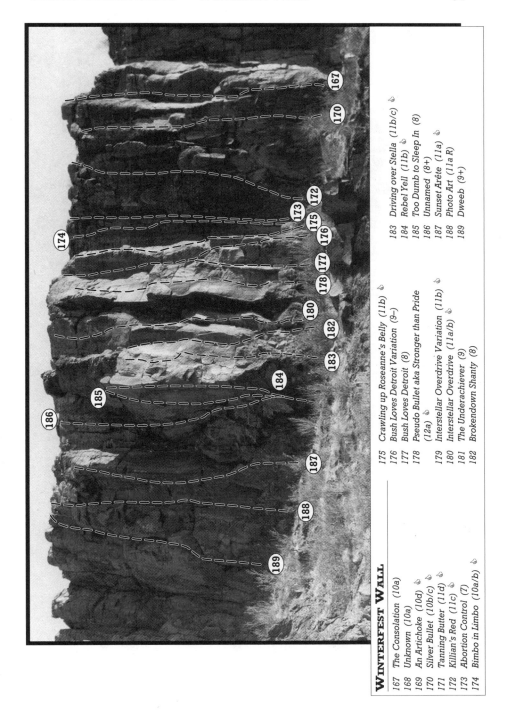

WINTERFEST WALL

167 The Consolation (10a)
168 Unknown (10a)
169 An Artichoke (10d)
170 Silver Bullet (10b/c)
171 Tanning Butter (11d)
172 Killian's Red (11c)
173 Abortion Control (7)
174 Bimbo in Limbo (10a/b)

175 Crawling up Roseanne's Belly (11b)
176 Bush Loves Detroit Variation (9–)
177 Bush Loves Detroit (8)
178 Pseudo Bullet aka Stronger than Pride (12a)
179 Interstellar Overdrive Variation (11b)
180 Interstellar Overdrive (11a/b)
181 The Underachiever (9)
182 Brokendown Shanty (8)

183 Driving over Stella (11b/c)
184 Rebel Yell (11b)
185 Too Dumb to Sleep In (8)
186 Unnamed (8+)
187 Sunset Arête (11a)
188 Photo Art (11a R)
189 Dweeb (9+)

RISK AREA

191   *Sinister Minister of Evil (5.11d)*
192   *Baby Beeper (10b)*
193   *Unnamed (7)*
194   *Handcrack (8)*

195   *Chimney Route (8)*
196   *This Bolt's for You (11a or 11d)*
197   *Risk of Infection (11b)*
198   *Serendipity (9–)*
199   *Not (10a)*
200   *The Perfect Ten (10a)*

201   *Unnamed (8+)*
202   *Daddy Dwarf (10d)*
203   *Mama Midget (10b)*
204   *Big Red Catcher's Mitt (10c/d)*
205   *Almost Left Out (8)*

RISK AREA

CHIP POWERS ON KILLIANS RED (5.11c).

PHOTO BY: PETER DONELAN.

RISK AREA

204   *Big Red Catcher's Mitt (10c/d)*
205   *Almost Left Out (8)*

DAVE GOTTENBORG ON RANCID 5.10B).

PHOTO BY: DEAUN SCHOVAJSA.

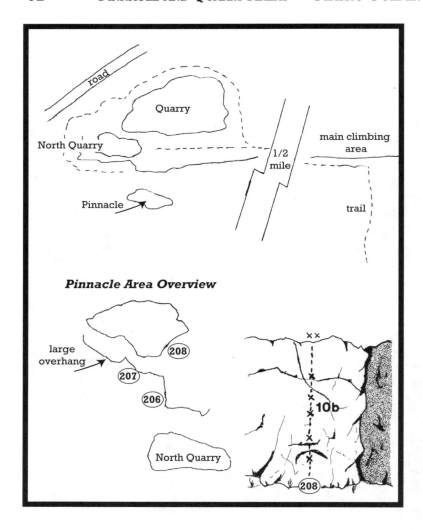

PINNACLE AREA

206   **Cracking Up (11b)**   Pro: Miscellaneous to 2 inches.
207   **Catching the Quarry (11a)** ♦

NORTH QUARRY

208   **Rancid (10b)** ♦   Pro: To 1 inch.

PINNACLE AREA
206 Cracking Up (11b)
207 Catching the Quarry (11a) 👆
NORTH QUARRY
208 Rancid (10b) 👆

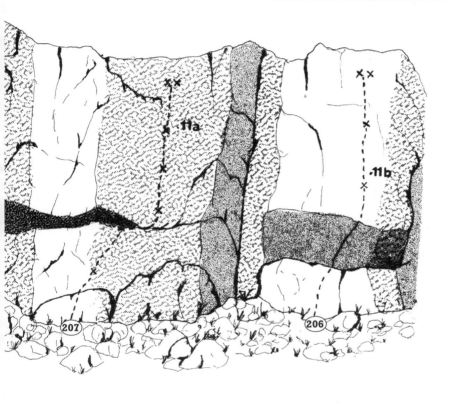

ROUTES BY RATING INDEX

*Ratings are rounded up, i.e. 5.10a/b is located under 5.10b. Abbreviations in parenthesis refer to areas: **BC** is Brown Cloud Crags; **CF** is Child Free Zone; **CS** is Cold Shut Area, **FA** is Fence Area; **HS** is Hot Spot Area; **IB** is Industrial Buttress; **NQ** is North Quarry; **OV** is Overhang Area; **PA** is Pinnacle Area; **RA** is Risk Area; **TP** is Twelve Pack Wall; **WF** is Winterfest Wall.*

5.6
- [ ] Kevin Spies the Line (OV)
- [ ] Killian's Dead ♦ (BC)
- [ ] Nipple Phyle (IB)
- [ ] Umph (OV)

5.7
- [ ] Abortion Control (WF)
- [ ] Conundrum, The (CS)
- [ ] Darker is Better (IB)
- [ ] For Love of Mother Not (CS)
- [ ] Honey, I Shrunk the Hemorrhoids ♦ (TP)
- [ ] How Rebolting (IB)
- [ ] Left-Hand Monkey Wrench (IB)
- [ ] Natural Fact (OV)
- [ ] Pack o' Bobs ♦ (OV)
- [ ] Thelma ♦ (BC)
- [ ] Thick Crust (BC)
- [ ] Unnamed (CS)
- [ ] Unnamed (RA)

5.7+
- [ ] Abortion Central (FA)
- [ ] Another Unnamed Billy Bob Route ♦ (OV)
- [ ] Blow Chow (IB)
- [ ] Redrum (OV)

5.8–
- [ ] Belly Up (IB)

5.8
- [ ] Almost Left Out (RA)
- [ ] Big Dihedral (BC)
- [ ] Brokendown Shanty (WF)
- [ ] Bush Loves Detroit (WF)
- [ ] Chimney Route (RA)
- [ ] Corniche (OV)
- [ ] Fast Boat to China ♦ (IB)
- [ ] Handcrack ♦ (RA)
- [ ] Heidi Hi (IB)
- [ ] Interface ♦ (BC)
- [ ] John Adams' Adams Apple (BC)
- [ ] Lemons, Limes, and Tangerines ♦ (BC)
- [ ] Louise ♦ (BC)
- [ ] Love, Sex, and the IRS (TP)
- [ ] Meat is Murder (OV)
- [ ] Off Line (OV)
- [ ] Pee on D ♦ (BC)
- [ ] Scarlett's Pulse (IB)
- [ ] Stoney Middleton (IB)
- [ ] Thunderbird aka Light Beer (IB)
- [ ] Too Dumb to Sleep In (WF)
- [ ] Unnamed (TP)
- [ ] Windy Days (BC)

5.8+
- [ ] Beer Drinkers and Hell Raisers (OV)
- [ ] Don't Pout 'cause Yer Down 'n Out (OV)
- [ ] G-Spot ♦ (FA)

☐ Mandela aka Leaning Pillar (IB)
☐ Mournful Mullet (IB)
☐ Quayle Eats Bush (HS)
☐ See You, See Me (TP)
☐ Sick Minds Think Alike ☙ (IB)
☐ Sleeper (OV)
☐ Unknown (OV)
☐ Unknown (OV)
☐ Unnamed (RA)
☐ Unnamed (WF)
☐ Wazup? (IB)

5.9–
☐ Bush Loves Detroit Variation (WF)
☐ Hodat? (IB)
☐ In Between the Lines ☙ (OV)
☐ Pump You Up (TP)
☐ Let's Wake Up Ronnie and Barb (OV)
☐ Serendipity (RA)
☐ Shut Down, Plugged Up, and
  Cold to Boot (CS)
☐ Spitfires and Funeral Parlors (TP)
☐ Unknown (CS)
☐ Variation (BC)
☐ Variation (OV)

5.9
☐ Brain Cloud ☙ (IB)
☐ Drinking Wine with the Chinese (OV)
☐ Fenced In (FA)
☐ Foul Play (FA)
☐ Hellraiser (OV)
☐ Honed to the Bone (Not!) (HS)
☐ Noodle Factory (IB)
☐ This Ain't Naturita, Pilgrim ☙ (OV)
☐ Underachiever, The (WF)
☐ Unknown ☙ (TP)

5.9+
☐ Briefcase Fulla Blues (TP)
☐ C'est le Morte (TP)
☐ Deck Chairs on the Titanic ☙ (BC)
☐ Dweeb (WF)
☐ Jell-O Brand Napalm (WF)

☐ Kid's Climb ☙ (BC)
☐ Mr. Coors Contributes to
  the Pink Stain ☙ (OV)
☐ New River Gorge
  Homesick Blues ☙ (BC)
☐ Nine to Five ☙ (HS)
☐ Polyvinyl Chloride (IB)
☐ Quark for Quayle, A (HS)
☐ Variation (OV)

5.10a
☐ Big Loose Goose (CF)
☐ Consolation, The (WF)
☐ Dumb Politicians (HS)
☐ Hellbound II (OV)
☐ Henry Spies the Line ☙ (OV)
☐ Louise Arête Variation (BC)
☐ Mechanically Inept (CS)
☐ Not ☙ (RA)
☐ Perfect Ten, The ☙ (RA)
☐ Politicians, Priests, and
  Body Bags ☙ (IB)
☐ Sidelines (OV)
☐ Tenacious ☙ (BC)
☐ The World thru a Bottle, The (HS)
☐ Thin Lizzie (WF)
☐ Toure Koundra (IB)
☐ Under the Wire ☙ (WF)
☐ Unknown (CF)
☐ Unknown ☙ (TP)
☐ Unknown (WF)

5.10b
☐ Baby Beeper ☙ (RA)
☐ Bimbo in Limbo ☙ (WF)
☐ Brown Cloud Arête ☙ (BC)
☐ Chunky Monkey ☙ (TP)
☐ D's Dry Dream ☙ (OV)
☐ John Roskelly Show, The ☙ (IB)
☐ Mama Midget ☙ (RA)
☐ Pass the Basalt, Please (FA)
☐ Rancid ☙ (NQ)
☐ Raw Fish and Rice ☙ (TP)
☐ Shadow of a Hangdog ☙ (IB)

5.12a

- ☐ Electrocuticles ☙ (FA)
- ☐ Handle this Hard On ☙ (OV)
- ☐ Insult and Flattery ☙ (FA)
- ☐ Mrs. Hen Places a Peck ☙ (OV)
- ☐ Pseudo Bullet aka Stronger than Pride ☙ (WF)
- ☐ Psycho Beta Buck Down ☙ (TP)
- ☐ Virus, The ☙ (BC)

5.12b

- ☐ Widespread Selfishness ☙ (HS)

5.12c

- ☐ Monkey Puzzle ☙ (CF)

5.12d

- ☐ Solar Panel ☙ (FA)

5.13

- ☐ Project (OV)

ROUTES BY NAME INDEX

Routes are listed alphabetically. Bolded numbers refer to topos or photos of the feature or route.

ACCESS: It's every climber's concern

The Access Fund, a national, non-profit climbers' organization, works to keep climbing areas open and to conserve the climbing environment. Need help with closures? land acquisition? legal or land management issues? funding for trails and other projects? starting a local climbers' group? CALL US!

Climbers can help preserve access by being committed to leaving the environment in its natural state. Here are some simple guidelines:

• **STRIVE FOR ZERO IMPACT** especially in environmentally sensitive areas like caves. Chalk can be a significant impact on dark and porous rock—don't use it around historic rock art. Pick up litter, and leave trees and plants intact.

• **DISPOSE OF HUMAN WASTE PROPERLY** Use toilets whenever possible. If toilets are not available, dig a "cat hole" at least six inches deep and 200 feet from any water, trails, campsites, or the base of climbs. *Always pack out toilet paper.* On big wall routes, use a "poop tube" and carry waste up and off with you (the old "bag toss" is now illegal in many areas).

• **USE EXISTING TRAILS** Cutting switchbacks causes erosion. When walking off-trail, tread lightly, especially in the desert where cryptogamic soils (usually a dark crust) take thousands of years to form and are easily damaged. Be aware that "rim ecologies" (the clifftop) are often highly sensitive to disturbance.

• **BE DISCREET WITH FIXED ANCHORS** *Bolts are controversial and are not a convenience*—don't place 'em unless they are *really* necessary. Camouflage all anchors. Remove unsightly slings from rappel stations (better to use steel chain or welded cold shuts). Bolts sometimes can be used pro-actively to protect fragile resources—consult with your local land manager.

• **RESPECT THE RULES** and speak up when other climbers don't. Expect restrictions in designated wilderness areas, rock art sites, caves, and to protect wildlife, especially nesting birds of prey. *Power drills are illegal in wilderness and all national parks.*

• **PARK AND CAMP IN DESIGNATED AREAS** Some climbing areas require a permit for overnight camping.

• **MAINTAIN A LOW PROFILE** Leave the boom box and day-glo clothing at home—the less climbers are heard and seen, the better.

• **RESPECT PRIVATE PROPERTY** Be courteous to land owners. Don't climb where you're not wanted.

• **JOIN THE ACCESS FUND!** To become a member, make a tax-deductible donation of $25 or more.

The Access Fund

Preserving America's Diverse Climbing Resources
PO Box 17010 Boulder, CO 80308
303.545.6772 • www.accessfund.org